Barbara Jordan:
Breaking the Barriers

Barbara Jordan:
Breaking the Barriers

by
Ann Fears Crawford

Halcyon Press Ltd ◆ Houston, Texas

Published by Halcyon Press, Ltd. www.halcyon-press.com

For information, write:

Halcyon Press, Ltd.
6065 Hillcroft Suite 525
Houston, TX 77081
info@halcyon-press.com

FIRST EDITION

Library of Congress Cataloging-in-Publication Data

Crawford, Ann Fears.
    Barbara Jordan : breaking the barriers / by Ann Fears Crawford. -- 1st ed.
        p. cm.
    Summary: Traces the life of this African American woman who was a respect-
ed lawyer, politician, teacher, and spokesperson for democracy. Includes biblio-
graphical references.
    ISBN 1-931823-11-1 (lib. bdg. : alk. paper)
    1. Jordan, Barbara, 1936-1996--Juvenile literature. 2. Legislators --United
States--Biography--Juvenile literature. 3. African American women legislators
--Biography--Juvenile literature. 4. United States. Congress. House--Biography
--Juvenile literature. 5. African American women legislators--Texas--Biography
--Juvenile literature. 6. Texas--Politics and government--1951- --Juvenile lit-
erature. [1. Jordan, Barbara, 1936-1996. 2. Legislators. 3. African
Americans--Biography. 4. Women--Biography.]
    I. Title.
    E840.8.J62C73 2003
    328.73'092--dc21
    [B]
                                                        2002014062

for

Isabella and Kate
Makayla Ann and Zachary
Margaret, William, and Emmy

and for
Nadine Rose Sauer
a proud heritage

Contents

Illustrations

Edward A. Patton, Barbara Jordan's great-grandfather
and member of the Texas House of Representatives
from 1890 to 1892
—courtesy of the Texas State Preservation Board

Preface

I will never forget the first time I met Barbara Jordan. Friends had sung the praises of the Houston woman who would take her seat in the Texas Senate. It was a historic day, for she was the first African-American woman elected to the Texas legislature.

I went to hear her sworn in. Crowds of admirers and friends had come to Austin to witness the historic event, and it was the first time I had heard Barbara Jordan speak. And hers was a voice that I—and millions of Americans—would never forget.

Hers was a voice that spoke out for justice for all. For all African-Americans, for all women, for all Texans. Hers was a voice heard in the legislature and then in the United States Congress. Hers was a voice speaking out for the Constitution during the impeachment of President Richard Nixon.

Then she came home to Texas. Her students at the Lyndon B. Johnson School of Public Affairs heard her voice, teaching, guiding them about ethics in government. Governor Ann Richards also heard that voice and appointed her ethics adviser to the governor's office.

And then that great voice was stilled. Barbara Jordan was gone from us, but no one who was ever touched by her life will ever forgot her. They never forget her speaking out for justice and equality, her firm belief in the Constitution.

Barbara Jordan

Many who knew her remember her humor. Her face breaking into a broad smile, her eyes crinkling, her joyous laugh. Barbara Jordan enjoyed life to the fullest—and what a full life she had.

It was filled with triumphs and many important "firsts." The political road she chose to take was not always an easy one, and hers was a life reflecting hardship and discrimination.

But Jordan overcame every obstacle, broke every barrier, to become the most admired Texas woman of the twentieth century. She stands as a role model for all—women and men, African-American, Anglo, and Hispanic.

Everywhere I speak about women in Texas, I am asked, "Tell us everything you know about Barbara Jordan," and I do. What a great pleasure it is to share memories of this magnificent Texas woman.

Here is her story.

—Ann Fears Crawford
Houston, Texas

Acknowledgements

Researching the life of Barbara Jordan has been an exciting experience and one that many people have shared with me. I owe a very special debt of gratitude to my former student, Janet Jette, now an attorney in California, for her paper "Reflections on a Representative," her project for a class in Women in Politics I taught in the 1970s.

Diane Pringle, a student in my seminar on Texas Politics and Society also explored Jordan's career and found her fascinating, as did Patricia Steinocher in my United States history class.

In my evening history classes at community colleges in both Austin and Houston, I have taught many African-American women, some starting their college careers, others returning to college for degrees. They have always been fascinated by Jordan, and many brought their daughters to class when I lectured on her and her career.

One group at Houston Community College insisted: "You need to write about her. Write her story just the way you tell it to us." So for them, and their daughters, I have tried to do just that. All of the comments of these students are part of the fabric of the story.

No one writes about the Texas Congresswoman without exploring Mary Beth Rogers's fine biography, *Barbara Jordan: American Hero*, and Jordan's autobiography, *Barbara Jordan: A Self-Portrait*, written with Shelby

Hearon. Both aided the author in exploring Jordan's life.

Librarians and archivists have been most helpful in aiding with research. Will Howard of the Texas Room, Houston Public Library, aided with research, as did Ralph Elder of the Center for American History and the staff of the Austin-Travis County Collection, Austin Public Library.

As always, super librarian Bill Hord of Houston Community College sees that articles and books are available for research, and my administrative assistant Felicia Vega keeps the Jordan files up-to-date and aided with research on the project.

Gathering photographs can be a time-consuming project, and many agencies and libraries helped with these. Credits under each photograph tell you who contributed the photo.

Barbara Jordan
—courtesy of the Barbara Jordan Archives, Robert J. Terry Library,
Texas Southern University

Chapter 1

Congresswoman from Texas

The young woman placed her hand on the Bible. She glanced around her. The people she loved most were watching her as she took the oath of office.

She saw encouraging smiles from her mother, her sisters, friends, and supporters. All had helped her get to this day. All were here to cheer her as they had done throughout her career.

It was a most historic day both for the nation and for Barbara Charline Jordan, African-American woman from Houston, Texas. It was a day she would remember all her life. January 3, 1972. The day she was sworn in as a United States Congresswoman from Texas. The first African-American woman from the South to sit in Congress.

In a solemn voice filled with emotion, she repeated the oath. The words had great meaning for her for she swore to uphold the Constitution of the United States.

The Constitution. She had studied it and debated it. Now it was hers to uphold and defend. Hers and her fellow members of Congress.

Now here she was taking on a new challenge. It had been a long journey to this day. Often a bumpy road. A road filled with sweet success—and often with bitter disappointment.

But from the beginning it had been a road well worth traveling. A road that began on February 21, 1936 in Houston's all-black Fifth Ward.

Her journey would take her from a warm circle of family and friends at Houston's Good Hope Baptist Church to graduation from Phyllis Wheatley High School.

Then the golden days when she found her voice as a winning debater at Texas Southern University and on to law School at Boston University.

Then she came home, back to Houston to practice law and enter the world of politics. Volunteering to work in the Kennedy-Johnson 1960 campaign. Speaking for the Democratic party. Helping to get out the vote.

Then friends and supporters encouraged her to run for the Texas legislature. After all, no African-American woman had ever sat in the Texas Senate or the House of Representatives. Maybe she would be the first.

But she lost. Not once but two times. A bitter disappointment for Barbara Jordan. She was used to winning.

Then she made an important decision. She would run one more time. This time for the Texas Senate. It was a difficult campaign, but she won. She knew the joy of winning and serving as the first African-American woman in the Texas Senate.

And, now, the dream fulfilled. Barbara Jordan would take her place in the United States Congress. It was her proudest achievement—Congresswoman from Texas.

Benjamin and Arlyne Jordan, Barbara's parents
—courtesy of Rose Mary McGowan (Barbara Jordan's sister)
through American Showcase Productions

4

Chapter 2

Black Child

Arlyne and Benjamin Jordan greeted their third daughter, Barbara Charline, on February 21, 1936. She joined her two older sisters, Rose Mary and Bennie, in the crowded brick house on Sharon Street in the heart of Houston's Fifth Ward. There Barbara's parents shared the house with her grandparents.

Proud grandparents Charles and Alice Jordan also greeted their new granddaughter. Everyone was pleased with the newest addition to the family.

It was her father, Ben, however, who expressed his amazement at his new daughter. She was so black. A dark-skinned child, while his other daughters were light-skinned.

To many African-Americans in the 1930s, light skin was a sign of beauty. They believed light-skinned African-Americans had more opportunities. Better chances for education and jobs. Better chances to "make it" in a world dominated by whites. Especially by Anglo males. But Grandpa John Ed Patten thought his new granddaughter was beautiful. A wonderful child, no matter what the color of her skin.

When Barbara was growing up, the two became special pals. By the time she was five, she was spending days playing in Grandpa Patten's junkyard. He made her his partner in the junk business and assigned her to help sort and bundle rags and newspapers. When Grandpa Patten sold them, he shared his profit with his partner, Barbara.

Growing up a tomboy, Barbara delighted in her junk-yard partnership. Grandpa Patten bought her a bicycle and even gave her a pair of "diamond" earrings.

Most important, he treated her like a true partner. He talked to her and listened to what he had to say. Grandpa Patten believed in Barbara Jordan and taught her to believe in herself. He made her know she could be whatever she chose to be.

Barbara and Grandpa Patten shared a special bond, and he often told her he wished she had been named from him instead of her other grandfather, Charles Jordan. When the two were together, he would laugh and call her "Barbara Ed-ine."

If Grandpa Patten was a joy for young Barbara, her father was often a problem. Ben Jordan was a strict parent, who wanted his daughters to grow up to be respected members of the community.

He demanded excellent schoolwork from each of them, and he was strict about what they could do and what they could not do.

Barbara often wished she could rebel, but she never dared. She was too afraid of her father. Living with her strict father, she learned to control her feelings and her actions.

But once she and her sisters did rebel—and with their mother's help. All three girls wanted to see a Shirley Temple movie but knew their father would disapprove. Their mother helped by having a cousin take them to see the movie. For Barbara, it was a great adventure, but not one she would think about repeating for many years.

Like many youngsters, Barbara could be mischievous and a problem in class. But one of her teachers at Atherton Elementary School told her aunt that she was misbehaving. All her aunt had to do was tell Barbara that she really hated to mention her behavior to her father. After that, Barbara Jordan was never a problem in school.

One of her teachers helped her understand that she was smart and could go far in the world. Barbara listened and learned. She studied hard and made good grades. But sometimes even her best work earned her a "B."

She might have all "A's" and only one "B," but her father would always ask her, "Why is this grade a 'B'?" Ben Jordan encouraged all his children to do their best and expected only the best from them. Later in her life, Barbara said that her father had a great influence on her.

Ben Jordan also helped with homework and went to his daughter's school programs. Barbara would remember him telling her, "I'll stick with you as far as you want to go." To her, the most important word in that sentence was "You."

For Barbara, it meant that her father was leaving the decision of what to do with her life up to her. And he would support her in whatever she wanted to do. It was important for her to have her father's encouragement and to know that he would be there for her.

The Jordan Sisters: Bennie, Barbara, and Rose Mary
—courtesy of Rose Mary McGowan (Barbara Jordan's sister)
through American Showcase Productions

Chapter 3

Fifth Ward

The world of young Barbara Jordan revolved around activities at the Good Hope Baptist Church in Houston's Fifth Ward.

In 1935, a year before Barbara was born, the Reverend Alfred A. Lucas became the church's minister. Reverend Lucas was a political activist and helped organize the Houston branch of the National Association for the Advancement of Colored People.

The NAACP was the major group working for civil rights for all African-Americans. Church members, plus others in the group, were determined that African-Americans would take their places alongside Anglos in education, the workplace, and the voting booth.

Working within the legal system, the NAACP challenged the Democratic party's white primary. In Texas the Democratic party was in control, and running in the primary, meant the candidate was elected.

During the 1940s and the 1950s, the NAACP won major victories in Texas. These victories—and others—would open the door of opportunity for African-Americans in the political world and would keep the door open until Barbara Jordan ran for the Texas House of Representatives.

Many NAACP meetings were held at Reverend Lucas's Good Hope Baptist Church, and Barbara met the world of politics at a very early age. Reverend Lucas also spoke about dignity and equality from the pulpit. His sermons carried a message to all African-Americans— work against segregation that kept African-Americans from enjoying equality.

Young as she was, Barbara heard the sermons and understood the message. She also played games with other children in the congregation. They would divide up into two teams—Christians and sinners. Barbara was always a sinner because she had not been saved.

She determined to do something about it. She had promised Grandpa Patten that she would not join the church until she was twelve years old, but she was tired of being a sinner. So when she was ten, she heard Reverend Lucas make the call for sinners to be saved. She stood up, marched down the church aisle, and made her statement.

With her father beaming proudly, she told the Reverend Lucas, "I want to join the church to be bap- tized and become a Christian." She was baptized into the church, and her strong Baptist religion remained important to her throughout her life.

Then, when Barbara was thirteen years old, her life changed. Her father felt the call to become a minister himself. Ben Jordan had attended Tuskegee Institute, founded by Booker T. Washington for the education of African-Americans. Although he didn't graduate, Ben had developed a deep, resonant speaking voice in college.

Now he sought his own personal salvation through the ministry and the need to take God's word to others. He became minister of the Greater Pleasant Hill Baptist Church in the Houston Heights area. Barbara's father's new job meant a move for the family, a move from the warmth and security of The Good Hope Baptist Church and the neighborhood where she had been born.

It meant a move to a new house too. No longer would the Jordan girls have the security of grandparents sharing their home and nurturing them. No longer would Barbara's childhood friends be close by. No longer would she be part of her old neighborhood.

Greater Pleasant Hill Church was a disappointment too. It was old and lacked the firm fellowship of Good Hope. It was hard for Barbara to accept her father as her minister, and religion became difficult for her.

Her home was also a disappointment. Instead of her grandparents' brick house, the family moved to a wooden house close to the railroad yards. Barbara was ashamed to tell her friends she lived on a street that was not even paved.

When Rose Mary went away to college, Bennie and Barbara formed a church singing group. The group performed at other churches in the Houston area, and Barbara began to recite poetry between songs.

One of her favorites was James Weldon Johnson's *The Creation*. The famous African-American poet captured the creation of the world just as a minister might preach a sermon. Time and time again, Barbara repeated Johnson's words, using her voice to make the words come alive:

> And God looked out on space,
> And he looked around and said:
> I'm lonely—
> I'll make me a world . . .

People applauded the group when they sang, and they applauded when Barbara recited poetry.

The best thing about the move was that Barbara got to attend Phyllis Wheatley High School, the best high school for African-Americans in Houston. Bennie had gone to the school the year before, and Barbara could

11

hardly wait to enroll. Now she would have more friends and take part in high-school parties and dances.

Barbara also took part in after-school activities at Hester House in her community. On Friday nights airmen from a nearby base would come to dance with girls at the canteen. Ben Jordan had forbidden his daughters to dance at the canteen, and Barbara didn't even know how to dance. But she loved the music and singing for the crowd.

Like most teenage girls, Barbara was also taking an interest in her looks. She curled her hair, wore jewelry, and longed to be a cheerleader. But cheerleaders at Wheatley were light-skinned girls, and she knew she'd never make the squad. It also disappointed her that teachers favored light-skinned students.

Many girls were using bleach to make their skin lighter, but Barbara wouldn't do that. Grandpa Ed Patten had taught her to have pride in herself.

She had her pride and her speaking ability. When she went to visit Rose Mary at college, the college girls would crowd around Barbara. She would tell them stories, using her voice dramatically, using gestures to accent her words. The college students loved her stories, and they loved her.

Barbara Jordan discovered that she had a voice. A deep, rich voice. A voice that could shake the rafters when she wanted it to. A voice that made people sit up and listen.

Barbara Jordan as a teenager
—courtesy of the Barbara Jordan Archives, Robert J. Terry Library,
Texas Southern University

Chapter 4

Speaking Out

When she was a sophomore at Wheatley, Barbara made an important decision. She was determined to become the best public speaker at Phyllis Wheatley High School.

Her teacher, Evelyn Cunningham, encouraged her to try for election as an attendant to Miss Wheatley. But Barbara knew she would never win. That honor went to light-skinned girls.

She set her goal even higher, and she could wait for it. She wanted the highest honor that could come to a senior—Girl of the Year. No one at school elected the Girl of the Year; the winner was chosen by a woman's group from among the senior girls.

All Barbara had to do was become the most outstanding girl in her class, and she knew how to do it. She told no one of her ambition, but she began speaking at every meeting and taking part in contests.

Speech teacher Ashton Jerome knew a winner when he heard one, and soon asked Barbara to join Wheatley's oratorical team. She won contest after contest, moving from local contests all the way to state competition. She brought home medal after medal to her high school. Her school was proud of her, and Barbara took enormous pride in her success. Then the greatest success was hers. She won first place in an oratorical contest with a trip to

15

Chicago for the national contest. Her travel was paid by the area's Baptist churches.

With her mother accompanying her, Barbara Jordan made her first trip out of Texas. She was excited as she dressed in her new pink evening gown, and even more excited as she stepped up to the podium at Chicago's Greater Bethesda Baptist Church.

She knew her speech by heart and knew it was a winner. And win she did. First place. She was thrilled and later said, "I was riding on a great big high."

Not only was she a winner in a national contest, she was well on her way to being Wheatley's Girl of the Year. Barbara was popular with both students and teachers. She had many friends, and they all attended football games to cheer their team on. She was a member of the All Girl's Choir, active in clubs, and president of the honor society.

Then in her senior year, the announcement came. Barbara Jordan was Wheatley's Girl of the Year. Everyone was so proud of her. And Barbara was proud of herself. But what would she wear to the awards ceremony? She hadn't even thought about a dress, and there was no money to buy one.

Aunt Mamie Reed came to the rescue, lending money for a new white lace dress, and Barbara liked the way she looked. She stood proud and tall as she delivered her acceptance speech. She had never been more pleased and excited in her life, and she knew her speech would be just what she wanted it to be—super!

When Reverend Lucas stretched out his hand and offered Ben Jordan a post at his church, Ben accepted. The Jordan family was back at Good Hope Baptist—and back to stay. Everyone was happy, but no one was happier than Barbara.

Barbara's life was great. Church, school, friends, and success as a speaker had made her life complete.

Then one day Edith Sampson came to speak to Wheatley students, and Barbara Jordan knew what she was destined to be in life.

Sampson was a lawyer, an African-American woman who had graduated from Loyola University in Chicago and had served as assistant state's attorney in Cook County, Illinois. She had also served as an alternate delegate to the United Nations.

Now she stood before the Wheatley students encouraging them to be lawyers. Barbara listened to everything Sampson said. She admired her poise, her self-assurance, the way she dressed. Edith Sampson was an impressive woman, and Barbara was impressed.

Right then and there in the Wheatley auditorium, two students decided they would become lawyers. One was Otis King, who would be Barbara's debate partner in college and later the first African-American lawyer in Houston. The other was Barbara Jordan.

Not everyone was as sure as she was. "Fine. We'll see." Her homeroom teacher dismissed her ambitions with these words. Her mother was also doubtful. Few women were practicing lawyers. Fewer still were African-Americans.

But Ben Jordan had encouraged his daughter to be all she could be. All she wanted to be. And the choice was up to her. Grandpa Patten also encouraged her. Barbara Jordan had made her choice. Now it was up to her to make her dream a reality.

Coach Thomas Freeman and his TSU
winning debate team
—courtesy of the Barbara Jordan Archives, Robert J. Terry Library,
Texas Southern University

Chapter 5

Star Debater

Now that Barbara had decided on her career, it was time to make a decision about college. She knew she did not want to go to Prairie View where Rose Mary had gone, so she decided to join Bennie at Houston's Texas Southern University.

Barbara made her decision based on the choices open to African-Americans at that time. She had not thought of choices in terms of the Anglo world. Sometimes she went to downtown Houston to shop. She went into five-and-dime stores to purchase school supplies, but she never thought about sitting at one of the stores' lunch counters.

Only Anglos could sit there and eat hamburgers and drink Cokes. Only Anglos could try on clothes in dress stores. To Barbara, it did not seem that this would change for a long time.

She didn't think it right, but for Barbara Jordan, high-school graduate, there seemed to be nothing she could do.

But by 1952 things were changing. TSU had a law school established by the state of Texas when African-Americans tried to enter law school at the University of Texas, and this was the school that Barbara chose to enter as an undergraduate.

Also the NAACP had sent attorney Thurgood Marshall to Texas. His job was to assault the Texas all-white primary in court. He won a significant victory in the case, *Smith v. Allwright*, and the all-white primary was declared illegal in Texas.

The NAACP went to court time and time again to challenge discrimination and segregation. They were determined to end "separate but equal" facilities for African-Americans. They, and many other African-Americans, knew that separate was—and never would be—equal.

Before entering TSU, Barbara had met the college's debate coach, Tom Freeman. When she came in second in a speech contest, he told her he had voted for her for first place. Now she was determined to look him up and win a place on TSU's debate team.

Barbara and Otis King, her high-school classmate tried out for the debate team at the same time. Tom Freeman chose them both and made them partners. Freeman was also an excellent coach, helping Barbara to perfect her speaking style. Soon Barbara was the team's most dramatic, most effective orator.

But Freeman had a problem with his female debater. Many of the tournaments were out of town, and the team would often drive all night. The coach did not want to take the responsibility for a young woman among so many men.

Barbara made a decision to change her looks. Her body had changed, as she had gained twenty pounds in her freshman year. She began to wear boxy jackets, skirts, and flat shoes. She cut her hair short. Now she looked much like the young men. People looked at her differently. Now it was all right to travel with the team.

This was a look that Barbara Jordan would keep for the rest of her life. While she gave up much of her femininity, she was accepted in the world of men.

Barbara and Otis King were winning tournament after tournament, but they were debating only African-American students. During their sophomore year, Freeman entered them in a tournament at Baylor University in Waco, Texas. For the first time in the South, a team of African-American students would debate Anglo students.

Barbara was excited and a little bit scared. Not only would she and Otis be debating, but Freeman had also entered her in the declamation contest. She would be going one-on-one against Anglo women. But Freeman had confidence in her; he knew she could win. And when the winners were announced, Barbara Jordan had won another first place award. And this time against Anglo women as well. Now her confidence soared.

Preparing for debates also taught Barbara important skills. She learned to research, to organize information, and to present that information effectively. And traveling with the debate team allowed her to see much of the country. By the time she and Otis were juniors, Freeman scheduled them to debate against teams from the University of Chicago, New York University, and even Harvard.

Coach Freeman's star debaters were making names for themselves, and the Harvard team came to TSU to debate them. Although the judges ruled the debate a tie, Barbara Jordan always considered it a "win."

Barbara Jordan with her parents and sisters
—courtesy of the Barbara Jordan Archives, Robert J. Terry Library,
Texas Southern University

Chapter 6

Becoming a Lawyer

During her senior year, Barbara began thinking about which law school she would attend. Harvard was the best in the country, and she thought about applying there. Then Tom Freeman advised against it. "Go to Boston University," he told her. Women had been admitted to the school since the 1840s, and African-American women often entered the law school.

Barbara told no one of her plans, but sent away for catalogs and application forms. She knew she had the qualifications. High-school Girl of the Year. Star debater. Member of student council. Editor of the college yearbook. Top grades.

But where would the money come from? Ben Jordan promised all he could afford. Rose Mary and Bennie were teaching and could send her spending money. But it would be a tight squeeze for the entire family. During her law school years, Barbara would always be short of money.

When she arrived at Boston University, she also found that she was short on experience. A world of culture—music, literature, and art—was open to Anglo students. A world that Barbara Jordan, a young African-American woman from Houston's Fifth Ward had never known.

There was no way she could catch up. She would just have to do what she had done before. Set her own goals and work toward them. She was also very lonely. No members of her family to encourage her. No members of her church community to make her feel warm and accepted. No Coach Freeman to spur her on.

She had her roommate, LaConyea Butler, and she met Issie Shelton, another young woman from Houston. Both were African-American, and Jordan longed for friendships among Anglo students, as well.

Her prayers were answered when she met Louise Bailey, whose father was chairman of the Democratic National Committee. Soon Barbara was inviting other students to have a cup of coffee, and her circle of friends grew.

Studies posed a problem also. When she first arrived, she had boasted to Issie Shelton that she would make Law Review, the law school honor society. After all, she had been elected Girl of the Year. When Issie laughed, Barbara became even more determined.

But studying for a legal career was totally different from high school or her undergraduate courses. Not only were the courses more difficult, students were expected to reason and analyze legal materials and cases. No longer could she memorize and give back to the teacher what she had learned. Her law school professors wanted to know the reasons behind problems and how she had reasoned to come up with solutions. "You had to think and read and understand and reason," she recalled.

Barbara Jordan was scared. Scared she'd flunk out of law school. Scared to let the other students know how difficult classes were for her. So she didn't study with them in the library. She found a quiet study room in her dorm, and every night, loaded with books and papers, she studied for hours.

These were hard times for Barbara, and times she would never forget. "I didn't get much sleep during those years. I was lucky if I got three or four hours a night, because I had to stay up. I had to."

Her first exam was in December, and Barbara was scared. Not only did she have to solve a problem, she had to reason through it. She had to show her professor how she had solved the problem.

She was scared as she took the exam, and she was scared when she finished. What if she failed? What if she flunked out? How could she write home to her father and tell him "I had busted out of law school"?

Grades would not be posted until after the Christmas holidays, and it was a sad time for Barbara. There was no money for her to travel back to Texas to be with her family. There was nothing to do but study, go to movies, and dread the day the grades were posted.

Although Louise Bailey called to wish her "Merry Christmas," Barbara was disappointed that her friend had not invited her to spend Christmas with her family. "I didn't expect that I was going to be tottling off to their big house," she remembered.

After New Year's the grades in criminal law were posted. She dreaded looking at the results, but there was her grade—79. She had passed. She had made it over the first law school hurdle.

Second semester would be easier. She joined a study group composed of other would-be African-American lawyers.

They helped one another by asking each other questions and talking through the cases they studied. Years later she remembered:

> You couldn't just read the cases and study alone . . . and you couldn't get it all in the classroom. But once you talked it out in the study group, it flowed more easily and made a lot more sense.

She finished her exams, but was exhausted. In addition, she was dreadfully homesick and longed to see her family. Ben Jordan found the money to bring his daughter home for a visit.

Barbara went home to Houston not knowing whether she had passed or failed. Then her final grades came, and she was excited. She had passed all her courses, and had gained a 78.4 average.

She went back to Boston ready for her second year, even more determined to succeed. Then one of her professors told her he knew she would make a good lawyer and sent her to talk with Edward Brooke. Brooke would later serve as United States senator from Massachusetts, and he and Barbara remained friends.

Her social world was opening up also. She made more friends and was doing better in her classes. She learned one valuable lesson—"You were a dodo if you were not prepared." And she resolved always to be prepared.

She also attended Sunday services at Marsh Chapel, drawn by the power of the preaching of the chapel's dean, Howard Thurman. He preached for the power of love and against racism in the world.

Thurman's preaching seemed very real to Barbara, and she often practiced his sermons at home. "God really is caring," she realized. "He just wants me to live right and treat other people right." It was a message that made good sense to Barbara.

Then her law school years were over. Although she had not made Law Review, she had passed. Her parents and sisters were there to watch her receive her diploma. Still she had to take the Massachusetts bar exam and thought about getting a job in Boston.

Then she received a phone call from her father. Grandpa Patten had been run over by a train and had lost his legs. No one knew if he would live or die. Barbara hurried to his bedside to hold his hand one last time. Her grandfather looked up at his special pal, the grandchild he had loved and nurtured, and then died.

Grandpa Patten had always held a special place in Barbara's heart. She remembered his making her a partner in his junkyard business and all the happy hours they had spent together. She especially remembered how he had found his "Barbara Ed-ine" to be a very special person and had faith in her. Now he was gone, but she never forgot him. To the end of her life, Barbara carried a picture of her grandfather with her.

Texas Senator Barbara Jordan reviews her mail
—courtesy of the Barbara Jordan Archives, Robert J. Terry Library,
Texas Southern University

Chapter 7

Running for Office

Houston in 1959 was a different city than the one that Barbara Jordan had left in 1957. When she had arrived in Boston, she had been amazed at its size. Now Houston was larger than Boston. It was a sprawling, wealthy city of booming businesses, choked freeways, and leafy suburbs.

But in many ways Houston had not changed. The Fifth Ward remained much the same, and Houston remained a segregated city. Although the Supreme Court had ruled that schools should integrate "with all deliberate speed," Houston students still attended all-Anglo or all-African-American schools.

The NAACP continued to work for equality for African-Americans, but little had changed. Barbara Jordan had lived in the East and seen that Anglos and African-Americans could live and work together. The South's treatment of African-Americans was one of the reasons that Barbara had considered living and working in Boston.

But how she was home, seeing old friends and preparing to take the Texas bar exam so she could practice law in her home state. When she passed the exam, she became the third African-American woman in Texas to become a lawyer.

But where would she practice? Who would her clients be? Her father helped by telling her to get business cards printed and to pass them out at church. Soon she had people seeking her out to draw up a will or to help get a divorce. She practiced law using her parents' dining room table for a desk.

Still she had time on her hands and an interest in politics. Before leaving Boston, she had become interested in the political career of Senator John F. Kennedy of Massachusetts. Now he was running for president with Texan Lyndon Johnson as his running mate.

When Barbara volunteered to work in the campaign, she was put to work stamping and stuffing envelopes, encouraging people to vote the Democratic ticket. But working the Kennedy-Johnson campaign put her in contact with Houston Democratic party leaders.

One of these was Chris Dixie, a founding member of the Harris County Democrats. Dixie was also a friend of many African-American community leaders and felt they should have prominent roles in Democratic politics. Dixie soon realized that Barbara Jordan could play a role in Harris County politics and put her to work with him.

One night a speaker failed to show. The meeting of block workers was in a church in the Fifth Ward, and Barbara was chosen to speak. Everyone listened, and even Barbara was amazed at the impact she had on voters. Party leaders saw the results of her speaking and put her on the speaking circuit.

Barbara Jordan was doing what she did best. Speaking out for candidates. Persuading people to vote. She was making her mark as a community leader, and people were beginning to notice her.

She loved what she was doing. She loved taking the word to African-Americans in the precincts, and Dixie saw to it that she spoke before Anglo voters also. She especially liked speaking to union members and in union halls. She felt she made a difference and convinced people that they could make a difference also.

Barbara Jordan was "bitten by the political bug," and she remembered that she "couldn't turn politics loose." She was disappointed that the Democrats lost Harris County in 1960, but pleased to see that the precincts she had helped organize voted strongly for the Kennedy-Johnson ticket.

Even after the campaign, she was in demand as a speaker. Later, she remembered:

> There was the novelty of my being a black woman lawyer, and graduating from a law school in Boston, and sounding different. That got attention.

Barbara Jordan was everywhere in Houston, speaking out on issues and working with Democrats. As a member of the Harris County Council of Organizations, she was helping to recruit African-Americans to run for office. But she wondered if an African-American woman could ever be elected to political office.

One campaign proved that an effective woman could win. African-Americans had organized their precincts, encouraged Democrats to pay their poll taxes, and were now recruiting candidates. They were determined to win a seat on the Houston schoolboard.

They found their candidate in Hattie Mae White, a schoolteacher and leader in the African-American community. White's campaign was the first time in Houston that Anglos and African-Americans worked together in a campaign, and her victory made politicians realize that African-Americans could win.

Chris Dixie was convinced that Barbara Jordan could win. Not just a local race. He encouraged her to try for a seat in the Texas legislature. But first Jordan needed a secure base in her precinct. She needed a law office. But where would she get the money?

She applied to colleges for a summer teaching position and was hired by Tuskegee Institute, the school her father had attended. She used her teaching money to open a law office in the Fifth Ward, sharing office space with two other lawyers.

Her father had given her a car when she graduated, and Jordan was soon recruiting clients like she had recruited candidates. "Our Barbara" the people of the Fifth Ward called her.

But Chris Dixie would not let her forget politics. He was determined that she should run for the Texas House of Representatives. The Harris County Democrats would pay campaign costs, and Dixie loaned her the filing fee. "Five crisp new one-hundred-dollar bills. And I liked that," she remembered.

Both Dixie and Jordan realized that in order to win, she would have to appeal to both Anglos and African-Americans. She had an Anglo, male opponent, Willis Whatley, who appealed to the conservative, business establishment. But Barbara Jordan had her powerful speaking voice and the Harris County Democrats solidly behind her.

Everywhere she went she talked about what Texas needed. She told voters she wanted to take some money from the University of Texas endowment fund and give it to poorer colleges, such as Texas Southern University and the University of Houston. She also promised to work to increase funding for welfare programs to help poor people and the elderly.

Jordan and Dixie knew she had a winning agenda, but conservatives were fighting hard against her. She lost! African-Americans voted for her, but she did not get the votes of Anglos.

Despite her loss, she knew she had to run again. Politics had become the most important thing in her life. She continued speaking out, especially for civil rights. She was a heroine and a celebrity to her friends in the Fifth Ward. But Barbara Jordan wanted more. She was determined to serve in the Texas legislature.

Then in 1963 she was in Austin to testify before a legislative committee on education. She stood in the gallery of the Texas House of Representatives and saw Willis Whatley in the seat where she had dreamed of sitting. "I ought to be in his place," she thought. "I deserve it."

Then in 1964 she challenged Whatley again. She had thought about running for another position, but another candidate convinced her to run against Whatley. She bought new clothes, and even a new car. She campaigned hard, speaking out on the issues. She was convinced she could win. However, on election day, she lost again. Although she had won 97 percent of the African-American vote and 50 percent of the Anglo vote, it was not enough. She had increased her total by 20,000 votes, but still she did not win.

Barbara Jordan didn't like losing, and she knew that she was—and could be—a winner. But she doubted that any African-American candidate could win in Houston. Maybe not in Texas. She even thought about leaving her home state. But Jordan knew that times were changing, and she wanted to be part of that change.

Texas Senator Barbara Jordan with fellow lawmakers
Rep. Bob Eckhardt and Rep. Curtis Graves
—courtesy of the Barbara Jordan Archives, Robert J. Terry Library,
Texas Southern University

Chapter 8

Working for Civil Rights

One evening Chris Dixie called Barbara Jordan and invited her to dinner. He told her that he and other labor members wanted to celebrate HER new civil rights. Jordan enjoyed laughing, eating dinner, and sharing political stories with Dixie, union members, and other liberals.

She also enjoyed celebrating her civil rights. The Civil Rights Act of 1964 held promise for all African Americans. Another Texan, President Lyndon Johnson was in office, and he was committed to civil rights for all Americans. Maybe change was possible.

Then, in 1965, Barbara Jordan became part of that change. Bill Elliott, a Harris County judge, offered her a job as his assistant. How could she refuse? She, Barbara Jordan, a woman lawyer from Houston's Fifth Ward, would become the first African-American to work at the courthouse in a position higher than a cleaning person.

It was an important opportunity, and Jordan knew it. So did the media. They ran stories about the new woman at the courthouse, and the new woman in Texas politics. Jordan knew how important her position was. She was the first African-American in an important position in any county in Texas.

She knew she could help people in Harris County. She looked at each county agency to see how it could work better, and she also helped people on welfare become working citizens. She was determined to make people's lives better.

Also her job helped her. She was able to expand her world by moving among Anglos. Judge Elliott even allowed her time off to give speeches and attend meetings. Now she was speaking out and meeting people all over Houston.

She knew that changes had been made, but thought there could be more. Students from TSU and civil rights leaders had staged sit-ins and protest marches. Now most of Houston's public facilities were integrated. African-Americans could eat in restaurants and try on clothing in stores downtown.

But the Houston schools were still separate. *Brown v. Board of Education* had been an important court case. The Supreme Court had ruled that schools should integrate "with all deliberate speed." Not only were schools in Houston not moving "with all deliberate speed," it seemed to Barbara Jordan they were moving at no speed at all.

Like many civil rights leaders, Jordan's aunt, Mamie Reed Lee, thought it was time for action. She took a member of her church, Beneva Williams, to an all-Anglo school to enroll. When Beneva and another student were denied the chance to go to the school they had chosen, the NAACP filed a court case.

The district court ordered the Houston schools to integrate, but still nothing happened. The NAACP went back to court, and this time the court ordered the Houston schoolboard to present a plan for integration of all schools.

The board moved to integrate only one grade at a time. Jordan and others thought the board was moving at a snail's pace. It would take many years for all grades to be open to African-American students.

Parents began pushing for civil rights. They asked the board to allow African-American students to attend vocational classes at an all-Anglo high school. The board put the program on hold.

Enough was enough. It had been more than ten years since the Brown decision. The time for integration had come.

Barbara Jordan was one of four African-American community leaders who signed a letter of protest, and the NAACP presented it to the board. When the board stalled again, they decided it was time for action.

Jordan and others formed PUSH—People for Upgraded Schools in Houston. They decided to follow the example set by the Reverend Martin Luther King, Jr. They planned a protest march to show the board the strength of the African-American community.

PUSH organized a boycott of the schools. African-American students would not attend Houston schools for one day. Instead they would join civil rights leaders to march from the South Central YMCA to the schoolboard building.

Many students did not choose to march, but did boycott school for that day. Others joined civil rights leaders to march, chanting, "All we want is freedom, and we want it now."

Board members agreed to meet with members of PUSH, and the United States Justice Department ordered them to integrate their schools through the twelfth grade by 1966. PUSH had done its work, and the Houston schools were integrated.

Once again Barbara Jordan had helped make a difference. In Washington President Johnson's administration was making a difference also. In 1965 Congress passed a Voting Rights Act that ruled that African-Americans could not be denied the right to vote. The government could monitor state elections.

The following year Congress ruled that requiring voters to pay a poll tax was also illegal. Poll taxes had kept many African-Americans and poor Anglos from voting. Another change in the laws also helped African-American voters.

In *Baker v. Carr* the Supreme Court ruled that each legislative district should be made of the same number of voters. Many people called this ruling the "one man, one vote" law, but Barbara Jordan knew it meant women also. And she might just be the woman to win a Senate race.

The Supreme Court also ruled that Texas would have to redraw its district lines. Each district would be based on population, and each district should have the same number of people.

One state Senate district included the Fifth Ward and other areas where Jordan had gained 50 percent of the vote. She had carried almost every precinct in the new district. The new Senate District Eleven seemed just made for Barbara Jordan.

Texas Senator Barbara Jordan
—courtesy of the Barbara Jordan Archives, Robert J. Terry Library,
Texas Southern University

Chapter 9

State Senator

Barbara Jordan began telling friends she would run for the Texas Senate. If she didn't win this time, it would be her last political race. Then Representative Charles Whitfield called. He tried to get her not to file. He was going to run and he was going to win.

Jordan knew he would be a powerful opponent. He was a member of the House of Representatives, and he had won his seat with the help of labor and liberals. Still Barbara told him she was in the race, and she would win.

Her friend Chris Dixie supported her, and so did union members. They knew that if Jordan won a seat in the Texas Senate, she would make history. For the first time in the history of the state of Texas, an African-American woman would hold a seat in the Texas legislature.

But Jordan had to quit her job. She couldn't run for state office while working for the county. Her former debate partner came to the rescue. Otis King offered her a job as a project director with the Crescent Foundation. When Jordan checked with the U.S. Labor Department, she found she could work on a federal project while campaigning for the Texas Senate.

And campaign she did. She knew it would be a fight all the way. First, she had to win the endorsement of the

Barbara Jordan

Harris County Democrats, as they had supported Whitfield for the House of Representatives.

Chris Dixie and other liberals helped win the endorsement for her. Then Whitfield asked the Justice Department to investigate her work with the Crescent Foundation, but Jordan had cleared it with the Department of Labor.

Whitfield sent messages into the African-American community. If they were truly devoted to civil rights, they would vote for an Anglo male. No way were the people who had supported Barbara Jordan in two races going to abandon her now.

Then Jordan won another important endorsement. The liberal *Texas Observer* carried an editorial supporting her. The editors argued that the barrier against African-Americans in the Texas legislature should be broken. They pointed out that Jordan was better qualified than Whitfield, was more liberal, and made better speeches. "Let us hope that Miss Jordan is elected," they wrote.

And elected she was, but not without a bitter fight. Still she had many supporters fighting by her side, and she sent out flyers to voters showing them exactly how to vote—and how to vote for her. She appealed to all voters in the district—"I need your help."

And help they did. Flocking out to vote and to get others to vote. Election day dawned on May 8, and Jordan worked hard visiting the polls where voters cast their votes. She then awaited the results of the Democratic primary.

When the votes were counted and the results were announced, Barbara Jordan was the winner—with 64 percent of the vote. She had no Republican challenger, so she was a member of the Texas Senate.

There was a huge party for her and her supporters. Her parents were joyful, and her sisters too. Jordan could hardly believe that all their hard work had paid off.

Judge Elliott told the media how happy everyone was. He said: "This is jut a first step for her. We will be hearing a lot more from Barbara Jordan."

Texas newspapers carried stories about her win. Time magazine and the *New York Times* featured her photograph, telling people across the nation that here was a woman making her mark on the political scene. No one was happier than Barbara Jordan, who told reporters, "It feels great, just great."

It felt great too when she took her oath of office on Janury 10, 1967. Standing in the Senate at the Texas State Capitol, her hand on the Bible, she repeated the oath that Lt. Governor Preston Smith announced.

Many eyes were on her. Not just her family and her supporters who had taken buses from Houston to watch her take the oath. They were watching from the Senate galleries. But she knew that people around the state and nation were watching her too.

She realized she was a part of Texas history. The first African-American woman to take the oath of office. What would she do? How would she perform in the Senate? After all, it was considered to be a club—a club made up of Anglo males.

Barbara Jordan knew all eyes were on her, but she never worried. She had been in politics for years, and she knew the way to win was through work. Also, she refused to let her race be an issue. She would use her intelligence and her charm to make her way in the Senate.

She studied Senate rules, got to know the leaders in both the Senate and the House, and made friends with her fellow senators. Still there were times when she was lonely.

Every morning when the Senate was in session, a group of political leaders ate at a round table in an Austin hotel. Many important issues were decided and deals made at this breakfast meeting. For months the lone woman in the Texas Senate ate her breakfast by herself at a table in the corner.

She made up her mind she had to become a member of the club. Lt. Governor Smith helped her when she asked for two committee assignments. One was State Affairs, which she knew to be an important Senate committee. Because labor members had voted for her, she asked to be on Labor and Management.

Smith pleased and surprised her. He made her vicechair of Labor and gave her a seat on State Affairs. And he assigned her to nine other committees.

She made the business of the Senate her business. She listened to what the conservatives had to say and studied the issues. But she voted most often with liberal members. She voted with them against a sales tax to be paid by people living in cities. She knew the tax would hurt her people in Houston.

But no senator or group of senators should take her vote for granted. Barbara Jordan had always been an independent thinker. She would study the issues herself and make up her own mind.

But she had no trouble making up her mind on the issue of a minimum wage. She aided Texas farm workers in their effort to get a minimum wage through a Senate committee, but failed. Still she had fought a tough fight, and the farm workers remembered.

Even while in the Senate, she continued to speak to groups about important issues. The most important was voting, and she took the lead in holding seminars to encourage African-Americans to vote. When one conservative senator tried to restrict access to voting by doing away with voter registration by mail, Jordan went to work.

She visited with ten other senators, explaining why the bill was bad for Texas and how it hurt people who could not take the time to go to their courthouses to register. All ten senators sided with her. She had effectively killed the bill before it ever reached the floor.

She was also making her way inside the club. When there were lengthy debates in the Senate, the Lt. Governor, who presided over the body, would often leave and designate another senator to preside. On March 21, 1967, Lt. Governor Smith handed the gavel to Barbara Jordan.

Cameras clicked and reporters scribbled in their notebooks. Jordan had made history once again. She was the first African-American woman in Texas history to preside over the Senate.

Her fellow senators were also getting to know the freshman senator from Houston. She attended parties, told jokes and listened to them, even went on deer hunts with the male members. She learned to play the guitar and took part in singalongs. Barbara Jordan was becoming part of the club.

She knew she had made it at the end of her first Senate session. Her fellow senators voted her their outstanding freshman senator and declared their admiration for her. An honor indeed for Barbara Jordan.

President Lyndon Johnson chats with Barbara Jordan
—courtesy of the Barbara Jordan Archives, Robert J. Terry Library,
Texas Southern University

Chapter 10

One Among Few

During her first term in the Senate, Jordan received a telegram from President Lyndon Johnson. He invited her to meet with him and other leaders at a conference on Fair Housing. Should she go?   She had only been in the Senate a short while, and she would have to miss a day.

"Go," others advised her. "A telegram from the president of the United States is a summons," and so she went. She was delighted to meet other civil rights leaders, including Roy Wilkins and Whitney Young. Delighted to hear the president's plans for getting fair housing for African-Americans.

But when President Johnson turned to her and asked, "Barbara, what do you think?" she was astonished. She wasn't sure what she replied. But newspapers noted her answer and the fact that the president had singled her out.

President Johnson also saw that she was appointed to the Commission on Income Maintenance to help get the minimum wage for poorer people in the United States, and shocked her mother by calling Jordan at home to discuss the bill. Arlyne Jordan was not used to answering her telephone to hear a voice say, "This is the president calling."

Jordan also introduced a bill in the Texas Senate to help with civil rights. It was the Fair Employment Practices Act, which outlawed discrimination in the workplace. And she was present in San Antonio when Texas governor John Connally opened HemisFair '68, the fair planned to promote the state of Texas.

With others, she was shocked and saddened when news reached the group of the death of Martin Luther King, Jr. She was even more shocked at the governor's response to King's death. "Those who live by the sword, die by the sword." She rushed back to Houston to be among her friends and supporters to mourn the civil rights leader.

When Governor Connally moved onto the national scene, Lt. Governor Smith became governor of the state. Jordan remained his friend, sharing his confidence, and she soon made friends with the new lieutenant governor, Ben Barnes.

Barnes made her chair of the Labor and Management Relations Committee, vice-chair of Legislative, Congressional, and Judicial committees, and a member of ten other Senate committees. He also saw that she met national Democratic leaders such as Bob Strauss, head of the Democratic party.

Then Texas was rocked with a scandal. State officals were charged with corruption, and Jordan was afraid for her friend Ben Barnes. But Barnes was cleared of any wrongdoing. While others got jail terms, Barnes continued as lieutenant governor. But legislators and other state officials demanded reform.

As her second term continued, Barbara Jordan could look back on a record of success. United Press International had named her one of the ten most influential women in Texas—the first African-American woman to receive the honor. She had also flown to

Houston on Air Force Two with Vice-President Hubert Humphrey when he came to Texas to give a speech.

What she was proudest of was helping many Texans get a minimum wage. She and Senator Joe Bernal of San Antonio worked together to pass the bill through the Senate. Although Jordan did not think the wage rate was high enough, many Texans would get $1.25 an hour. Farmworkers and laundry workers, many of them African-American and Hispanic, would get the minimum wage, and that made both the bill's sponsors proud.

She had also helped pass a worker's compensation bill. At last injured workers would receive part of their pay when they were injured and could not work. Many business leaders opposed the issue, but labor supported the bill.

Some senators thought benefits should be higher; others thought the bill did not go far enough. Jordan agreed, but she had learned to compromise. She knew the bill was the best she could get from conservative leaders. She had given them her word. A compromise had been reached, and she stuck by it. The bill passed with no amendments.

Liberal leaders criticized her, but Jordan knew she had done the best she could. She told newspaper reporters that this might not be the best bill, but it was the best bill she could get passed through the Senate. She was glad when the bill also passed the House of Representatives and Governor Smith signed it into law.

As soon as she finished one fight, she was plunged into another. She joined with twenty-three liberal senators in a historic filibuster. They were determined that Texans should not pay a tax on food. Business leaders wanted to pass the tax to raise money for the state, but liberals knew it would hurt poor people.

Lt. Governor Barnes supported the bill, but Jordan and other liberals were determined to talk the bill to death. They would follow one another in talking, each taking a turn to oppose the bill. Senate rules allowed them to talk for as long as they could. When one senator grew tired, another took over.

Jordan took her turn, speaking for an hour without stopping. She told senators she did not understand why food for farm animals was not part of the bill. Food for people was. Why should horses be exempt? Why was baby food a part of the bill?

Still the conservatives had the votes, and the bill passed the Senate. But by a close vote, with Jordan voting against it.

Newscasters told Texans about the "bread tax." Newspaper stories told them about the Senate action and that now the bill went to the House of Representatives. Texans were angry.

They wrote and called their state representatives. They urged them to vote against the bill. Many consumer groups protested; Texans drove to the state capitol. They stood outside their representatives' offices and flooded into the House chamber. They threatened to boycott supermarkets and grocery stores, and the bill failed to pass the House. Texans had led a tax revolt and won.

Barbara Jordan was not only becoming a power player in Texas politics, she was making new friends. She met many women in Austin and often sang and played her guitar with them. Often her sisters and other Houston friends would join the group. Jordan was having fun and enjoying her life.

Then Ben Barnes appointed Jordan as vice chair of a committee to draw up boundaries for a new Congressional district in Houston. Houston had more people, and more people meant a new district. Each district must conform to "one man, one vote," and each district must have an equal number of people.

When the Senate finished creating the new Congressional district, it turned over the work of creating Senatorial districts to the Legislative Redistricting Board. When the lines were drawn, Jordan's Eleventh Senatorial District was changed. No longer would the district be primarily African-American.

One member of the House of Representatives complained. Curtis Graves had come to the House when Jordan won her Senate seat. Everyone knew he planned to run for Jordan's place when she moved on.

"She has sold us out," he told the press. The Eleventh District now contained fewer African-Americans, and he knew he could not win the Senate seat. He claimed that Jordan planned to run for Congress, and that African-Americans would lose their voice in the Texas Senate.

Not only did Graves speak out in the press, he filed a lawsuit in federal court. He charged that the board had deliberately drawn the lines so that no African-American could win. Jordan also doubted that an African-American could be elected from her old district, but the Supreme Court found that African-American voting strength in Harris County would not be less.

Knowing he could not win a seat in the Texas Senate, Curtis Graves made a decision. If Barbara Jordan filed for the new Congressional seat, he would file against her. And Jordan had decided to file. She wanted to make a difference on the national scene, and she thought the Congressional seat was hers.

President Johnson told her: "Don't go for it unless it's already in your pocket." Now with Graves in the race, she wasn't sure. This time Barbara Jordan knew she was in for the political fight of her life.

Judge Andrew Jefferson swears in Barbara Jordan as
"Governor for a Day"
—courtesy of the Barbara Jordan Archives, Robert J. Terry Library,
Texas Southern University

Chapter 11

Running for Congress

If Jordan was going to win her Congressional race, she needed money. Her supporters planned a huge fundraiser in her honor. It was to be a gala affair in downtown Houston, and Jordan had a new gown, a lovely hairdo, and an orchid corsage.

Her sisters, family, and friends would be by her side, and they were expecting a large crowd—many of the people with money who contributed to Democratic political campaigns.

Ben Jordan, however, would not be at his daughter's side. The parent who had always supported and encouraged her had heart disease. He was too ill to attend the fundraiser.

Another of her supporters, however, was there. Jordan had introduced President Johnson at another fundraiser. He told her, "I'm going to help you in whatever I can." Now Jordan asked for his help, and he came.

Surrounded by friends, Jordan greeted the former president with a big smile. Then he threw his arms around her in a big Texas-size embrace. They walked through the crowd together, greeting people as they went.

When he spoke, President Johnson reminded people of his support for civil rights. He reminded people of how difficult the fight had been. And then he talked about Barbara Jordan. He reminded the guests that they could vote for Jordan and feel good about their vote. He told the crowd:

> Barbara Jordan proved to us that black is beautiful before we knew what that meant. She is a symbol proving that We Can Overcome. Wherever she goes all of us are going to be behind her.

Jordan rose to thank the former president. She told him, "Mr. President, you make us all feel like first-class Americans." With the president's help, Jordan raised money to fund the campaign.

Still, Jordan had to face a tough election against the flamboyant Curtis Graves, who was determined to beat her. He would run a no-holds barred campaign. While he often resorted to slams against her, Jordan resolved not to run a bitter campaign. She was determined never to show her anger, no matter what Graves said. Instead, she ran on her record. As she told one group, "You must be part of the decision-making process. The issue is, who can get things done."

Houston's newspapers endorsed her, and Jordan and her advisers felt that the election was in the bag. Still she took her message to her supporters. She wanted them to know the issues and how she felt about them.

She decorated her campaign office in red, white, and blue and tacked up her photograph. She wanted everyone in the Fifth Ward to know who their candidate was. Volunteers nailed up campaign signs throughout the district. She took full-page ads in Houston newspapers.

She was endorsed by the Harris County Council of Organizations, but had difficulty with the Harris County Democrats. They demanded she support Democrat Frances Farenthold for governor of Texas. Her friend Ben Barnes was also running, but she needed the support of the Harris County Democrats. She agreed to support their entire Democratic ticket, and she won their endorsement.

On election night, she found that all her hard work paid off. She won her Congressional seat with 80 percent of the vote and also won 90 percent of the African-American vote in her district. All her friends and supporters gathered to celebrate her victory. When she was asked how she felt about her win, she told reporters, "It shows that black people want representatives that get things done."

Before leaving for Washington, there was one more duty that she had to do. That was to say goodbye to the members of the Texas Senate. The group where she had made political history.

When the legislature met in special session that spring, Lt. Governor Barnes made Jordan president pro tem of the Senate, and senators saluted her as their Governor for a Day. Both Governor Smith and Barnes left the state for a day, so that Jordan could serve as governor of the state of Texas—if only for a day.

And what a day it was! On June 10, 1972, crowds of family and friends swarmed to the state capitol. Buses carried high-school and middle-school students; the TSU choir sang; the band from Phyllis Wheatley High School played. Businesses in Houston's Fifth Ward closed for the day; everyone was in Austin to honor Jordan.

Many politicians honored her with their words, but Jordan's words reflected her thoughts on that important day. She told people she had thought about Houston's Fifth Ward and asked, "Who would have thought ten years ago that a product of Phyllis Wheatley High School and Texas Southern University would become governor of Texas, even for a day?"

Jordan received a standing ovation, and when she looked up into the gallery, she saw many people crying.

Helped to his feet, Ben Jordan, with tears in his eyes, applauded his daughter.

Tragedy struck, however, soon after the ceremony. When her father was leaving the state capitol, he collapsed. When she was shaking hands with guests at the reception, her sister Rose Mary told her that her father had been rushed to the hospital.

She had wanted this to be a glorious and happy day for her supporters, so she told no one about her father's illness. She enjoyed the barbecue held on the capitol grounds in her honor. She listened to the choir sing and the bands play. She watched Houston kids do the bugaloo on the capitol steps. But all the time her thoughts were with Ben Jordan.

As soon as she could, she left to join her mother and sisters at her father's bedside. The doctors had little hope; Ben Jordan had suffered a stroke. Knowing that her father was near death, his daughter leaned close to her father and said, "Chief, you almost made the day. But you got to see me be governor."

Later that evening, Ben Jordan sank into a coma. With his wife and daughters near him, Ben Jordan died and was taken to Houston to be buried. Barbara Jordan was there with her mother and sisters at Good Hope Baptist Church for her father's funeral. On that sad day, her mother told her what her father had said to her about their youngest daughter being Governor for a Day: "I wanted to see THIS DAY . . . that Black Girl."

Barbara Jordan enjoyed playing her guitar for friends
and supporters
—courtesy Houston Metropolitan Research Center, Houston Public
Library

Chapter 12

Member of the House

In the general election Jordan had only a token opposi-
tion from a Republican, Paul Merritt, so she did not
have to campaign as hard as she had in the Democratic
primary. She won the election on November 7, 1972
by 85,000 votes to Merritt's 19,000. The African-
American woman from the Fifth Ward was now a member of the United States House of Representatives.

The media took notice of her election. She was pho-
tographed for national magazines. The national press
wrote stories about the first African-American woman
from the South to sit in the Congress of the United
States.

Then she received a call from former president
Johnson. Members of the president's administration
were coming to Austin for the opening of his civil rights
papers. There would be speeches, talks, and discussions
about civil rights. President Johnson wanted Barbara
Jordan to be at the LBJ Library for the meetings.

The former president reflected on his administration
and his Great Society. He told the audience that there
were 31,000,000 papers in his presidential library. The
ones he valued the most were those about civil rights.
He felt that his greatest gift to the nation was the Civil
Rights Act of 1964, and Jordan agreed.

Before Jordan left the meeting, she and President Johnson walked over to view Lincoln's Emancipation Proclamation. They stood side-by-side to look at the document which had been brought to the LBJ Library for the meeting.

The proclamation reminded Jordan of the long, hard road that lead to civil rights for all Americans. It also reminded her of the responsibility she had as a representative of the people in her Congressional district.

Before taking her seat in the U.S. House of Representatives, Jordan went to Harvard University for the Congressional "Head Start" program. She was there with other freshman members of Congress to study at the John F. Kennedy Institute of Politics. They learned about federal agencies and bureaus and to study what a member of Congress does.

One of the things she learned was to make requests for committee assignments early and to consider carefully on what committees she wanted to serve. The Congressional Black Caucus wanted Jordan to serve on the Armed Services Committee.

She was a lawyer, however, and felt she might want to serve on the Judiciary Committee. Both were major committees, and she had to decide. Freshman members of Congress did not get two major committees.

Jordan asked former President Johnson to help her decide. He gave her some good advice. He said that the defense budget was always a problem. Everyone argued about it. It was not the best place for a freshman Congresswoman to be.

His suggestion was that she ask for the Judiciary Committee. He told her that if ever she lost her seat in Congress, she could always be a judge. This seemed a good idea to Jordan.

She asked to be on the Judiciary Committee and was pleased when she got it. She was also pleased that she was the first person named. But being a member of the House of Representatives was different from being a member of the Texas Senate.

In the Senate, she was one of thirty-one senators. It was easy to make a place for herself. Now she was one of 435 members. How could she make a difference? How could she make the members of her district feel they were important?

Jordan knew that she was the "new kid on the block," and that her first job was getting to know her fellow members. U.S. Congressman Bob Eckhardt from Houston helped by giving a reception for her. Texans in Washington and former students from TSU gave another. She was getting to know people in Washington, and they were getting to know the new Congresswoman from Texas.

She learned that women had never been allowed to attend the Texas Democratic Delegation Luncheon. She knew she had to be part of this group, and she was soon accepted. She broke through yet another barrier against women. She was proudest of the fact that her fellow Texans in Congress elected her secretary of the Texas delegation.

She soon became a member of the Black Congressional Caucus and was proud of being one of three women in the group. Barbara Jordan, Yvonne Braithwaite Burke from California, and Shirley Chisholm of New York were the three African-American women members of Congress.

Another member of the Caucus was Andrew Young of Georgia, who had worked with Dr. Martin Luther King, Jr. and was from the South also. He and Jordan knew the responsibility they held as the first African-American members of Congress from the modern-day South.

Caucus members were not pleased that Jordan had chosen the Judiciary Committee over their choice for her, the Armed Services Committee. They were also not pleased with her choice of a seat in the House. They sat together on the left side of the House. They thought Jordan should be with them.

But not Barbara Jordan. She chose to sit on the center aisle where she could hear and be seen. Here she could catch the eye of the Speaker of the House. And here people could easily stop to talk and visit with her.

However, she sided with the Caucus on their choice of a chairman of the Democratic National Committee. Bob Strauss of Texas was running for the post, and he counted on Jordan's vote. Then she told him she was sorry but she couldn't vote for him.

The Black Caucus did not like the fact that Strauss was close to John Connally. The former Texas governor had opposed the Civil Rights Act of 1964.

Then once again Jordan received sad news. President Lyndon Johnson had died at his Hill Country ranch. Barbara Jordan had lost not only a friend, but a political ally. She remembered all his kindness to her, his good advice, and his help to her with members of Congress.

She stood on the floor of the House of Representatives to speak about the former president. She told members of Congress how proud she was to count her fellow Texan as a friend:

> The death of Lyndon Johnson diminishes the lives of every American involved with mankind. The depth of his concern for people cannot be qualified. Black Americans became excited about a future of opportunity, hope, justice, and dignity. Lyndon Johnson was my political mentor and my friend. I loved him and I shall miss him.

Barbara Jordan was settling into her role as a member of the House. She was also working harder than other members, often staying late at her office. With her staff, who called her "BJ," she worked on legislation important to the people back home in Texas. She said of her job, "I am here simply because all those people in the Eighteenth District of Texas cannot get on planes and buses and come to Washington to speak for themselves."

One of the groups she spoke out for were the elderly women in her district. When Ben Jordan died, her mother found that her husband's Social Security benefits were not enough for her to live on. She had no benefits be-cause she had been a homemaker all her life.

Jordan teamed with fellow Congresswoman Martha Griffith of Michigan to sponsor a bill to provide Social Security benefits to homemakers. The bill failed, however, and it was not until the 1990s that homemakers received Social Security benefits.

Jordan was becoming interested in issues related to women and the elderly. She was also interested in seeing that her amendment requiring police departments to hire more minority officers passed and celebrated when it did. However, soon her time and efforts were absorbed by a crisis that threatened the Constitution of the United States.

Congresswoman Barbara Jordan listens to the
testimony of the House Judiciary Committee
—courtesy of the Barbara Jordan Archives, Robert J. Terry Library,
Texas Southern University

Chapter 13

Impeachment

Everyone in Washington was talking about a problem called Watergate. Newspaper and television reporters carried stories about the issue. Was President Richard Nixon involved? Members of Congress were worried, and one of those who worried most was Barbara Jordan.

President Nixon had been reelected to office by a huge majority of American voters. But burglars had broken into Democratic headquarters in the Watergate building. As more stories were printed, people began to feel that President Nixon and his office had known about the burglary. Could they have been part of it?

Jordan and other members of Congress were upset with the president for other reasons. He had refused to spend money granted to programs by Congress. He had cut programs set up by Congress. Many education programs depended on these funds. Many people in Houston's Fifth Ward needed these funds also.

President Nixon's actions threatened the Constitution. This document detailed the separation of powers in the government. The president did certain things; Congress did others. Now the president was taking over Congress's role.

Jordan and her fellow freshman members passed a resolution and spoke out on the floor of the House against the president's actions. Jordan spoke about her belief in the U.S. Constitution and against the president's taking powers that belonged to Congress.

Still the Watergate problem continued. Jordan, however, did not think charges of impeachment would be brought against the president. "You're talking about the presidency," she said. "You're not going to impeach the President."

Charges, however, were brought against the president. These charges would be heard before the Judiciary Committee, with Jordan sitting as a member. She would play an important role in the hearings to impeach the president.

The chairman of the committee, Peter Rodino, said of Jordan: "She began to display the ability to be concise and precise, but not aggressive. She was one who sat and listened."

Jordan also studied and read everything she could find about impeachment. She knew that a president could be impeached only for "high crimes and misdemeanors," but she wanted to know more.

Committee members studied the issues behind closed doors, and then the chairman opened their meetings to the media.

Each committee member could make a statement to the media, and Jordan had studied the issues. She knew she was going to speak in favor of impeaching the president. But she wasn't sure what she was going to say. She and her staff worked to make her statement just right.

On July 25, 1974, the television cameras turned on Barbara Jordan. Reporters sat with their pencils poised. Jordan knew people in Houston were listening, and she had her notes before her.

She looked directly into the camera and began to speak. "'We The People'," she said, quoting from the opening lines of the Constitution. She told listeners that when those lines were written in 1787, she was not included in 'We The People.'

She said she thought for many years that George Washington and Alexander Hamilton had left her out by mistake. But she felt that through amendments and court actions she was now included in 'We The People.'

She told listeners that this was a very solemn time. Impeaching a president was not an easy task. But she said, she believed in the Constitution of the United States. People across the nation remembered her words: "My faith in the Constitution is whole. It is complete. It is total."

Then Jordan told them she could not sit by and see the Constitution destroyed. No president or any other official could betray the public trust and not be removed. She pointed out that while the House of Representatives could impeach the president, it was up to the Senate to try him and decide whether to remove him from office.

Jordan pointed out that the committee had evidence that the president had known that money was paid to the burglars. He had met with people involved in the Watergate affair. The committee had found that the president had betrayed the public trust.

People listened. The media wrote and spoke about her words. The *Texas Observer* wrote of her: "Where did the voice come from? Like everything else about Jordan, it was always there." People across the nation wrote letters and sent telegrams. One nine-year-old girl wrote to agree with her and said, "I think you should run for president."

A "white, Yankee, Republican" added his support, telling her he would be honored to campaign for "our 1st black, 1st woman President," if she were the candidate. An immigrant to the United States wrote: "When you speak of that great Document 'the Constitution of our beloved United States' it brings tears to my eyes," while a woman congratulated her on fighting for American principles, saying, "God Bless you Honey! You were wonderful! I never was more proud of womanhood than in her shining hour."

When Barbara Jordan next went to Houston, she saw twenty-five billboards around the city, paid for by one citizen. They read: "Thank you, Barbara Jordan, for explaining the Constitution to us." Nothing made her more proud.

Still voting to impeach the president was hard for her. When the first article came up for a vote, she could hardly say "yes." The vote passed, but several members of the committee had to leave the room. It hit Jordan hard, and tears ran down her face. Others members cried also, but they had done their job.

The committee voted articles of impeachment and House members had to carry the articles to the Senate. Jordan decided she had to be one of those members, but she never got a chance. Knowing that he would be impeached and removed from office, the president resigned.

Then Jordan faced another hard decision. The Senate had to confirm Vice-President Gerald Ford as president of the United States. Jordan did not believe he would make a good president and voted not to confirm him.

Still Ford became president and invited Jordan to go to China. Other members of the Senate were also going. President Nixon had opened relations with China, and the group was to assure them relations with the U.S. would continue.

Jordan thought about the trip. She knew it was important, but China was far away. She thought about the trip for several days and decided to go. It was too important a journey to turn down.

As soon as the group got to China, they traveled to a small village at the foot of a mountain. Jordan was sleeping on a slotted cot with straw mats, when there was a knock on the door.

There was a telephone call for her all the way from Houston. A television reporter wanted to know what she thought of President Ford's pardon of Richard Nixon.

What did she think? She had no idea what the reporter was talking about. She asked him to repeat what he had said. Yes, it was true. The former president had been pardoned. Now there would be no court trial. There would be no resolution to the presidential crisis. That was the end of impeachment. For Barbara Jordan, it was a sad end to Watergate.

Former President Jimmy Carter and Barbara Jordan
—courtesy of the Barbara Jordan Archives, Robert J. Terry Library,
Texas Southern University

Chapter 14

Voting Rights

With the presidential crisis over, Barbara Jordan had to face a personal one. For some time she had been having health problems. Before the Watergate hearings, she had tingling feelings in her feet.

She knew her weight was a problem and tried wearing low-heeled shoes. Then her hands began to tingle too. Her doctor suggested more tests, but Watergate was her priority. Also, she did not want to lose her perfect attendance record in Congress.

Then she felt like pins and needles were shooting through her hands and feet. It was time for tests. Doctors suspected that Jordan had multiple sclerosis. No one knew what caused it, but there was no cure. Jordan faced the fact that she might become disabled.

What was she going to do? What could she do? Doctors prescribed drugs, but no one knew when the next attack might come. And it seemed that the disease would only get worse.

One drug made her feel better. She had more energy and her legs were stronger. She did not miss one of the Watergate hearings. Nevertheless, Jordan had a problem that would not go away.

She made up her mind not to let pain interfere with her work. She knew the disease would not go away, but she would not let it show in her work or in her private life. Her staff was sworn to secrecy; the disease was something only Barbara Jordan could deal with.

She won reelection to Congress and was becoming a celebrity in Congress. People wondered what she might do next. Would she become Speaker of the House? Had she set her sights on the Supreme Court? What about Barbara Jordan for vice president of the United States?

Some members of the House felt that she had her eye only on powerful positions. It was not Barbara Jordan's way to wait for others to make the right moves. She was always in the forefront and believed that power was a part of politics. "There is no place for women to be shy and retiring if they want to be leaders," she said.

And the time to use power came with one of the most important pieces of legislation—the Voting Rights Act. The act had been one of the most important pieces of civil rights legislation, and now it was time to extend the act.

In 1975, when the Voting Rights Act had been passed, Texas was not part of it. Only the Deep South was covered. The act was designed to remove obstacles and allow African-American voters access to the polls. Now it was time for the act to be reviewed, and Jordan knew that Texas had to come under the act.

Public officials in Texas did not want any changes in the voting process. In 1975, however, Jordan introduced a bill that would bring Texas under the act. Many Texans were Hispanic, and she also included a provision for ballots to be printed in both Spanish and English.

If voters were discriminated against, the federal government could send in registrars to conduct elections. Both African-Americans and Hispanics were protected under the law.

Texas legislators voted to print their ballots in both Spanish and English, but they opposed having their state under the Voting Rights Act. Texas filed suit to prevent any action, but the Supreme Court ruled that Texas must come under the act.

Jordan flew back to Washington when President Ford signed the bill. She knew he had opposed it, and her victory was too good to miss. When the president read his speech from cards, Jordan complimented him. "Your remarks were quite interesting," she told him. President Ford gave her his cards to remember the occasion, and Jordan was proud to have them.

Democratic party chairman introduces speaker Barbara
Jordan at the 1976 Democratic National Convention
—courtesy of the Barbara Jordan Archives, Robert J. Terry Library,
Texas Southern University

Chapter 15

Grand Slam Democrat

As the new year opened in 1976, Barbara Jordan found she was a celebrity. The Gallop poll named her as one of the twenty people that Americans admired most. She had lost weight, but her feet continued to bother her. She was terrified that she might trip and fall in public.

She began to doubt her future. She was frustrated by the debate in Congress on the Hyde amendment that would limit federal funds for abortions. When the debate grew too much for her, she told one of the women House members: "I'm going to the ladies lounge and read a book, and if you need me in this debate that's where I'll be."

She knew she was a media figure, and still she tried to hide the effects of her illness. Jimmy Carter, the governor of Georgia, had asked her to support him, and she agreed. However, when Bob Strauss, chairman of the Democratic National Committee, asked her to be one of the keynote speakers at the Democratic convention, she wondered if she would ever make it to the platform.

Even before the convention, rumors began that she might be the vice president, but Jordan did not take them seriously. What she did take seriously was her speech. She knew that she, the first African-American woman ever to speak before the convention would have to be at the top of her form. Her speech had to set just the right tone for people at the convention and the television audience.

The delegates at the convention were a noisy bunch. Even when former astronaut John Glenn began to speak, they continued to talk. Jordan wondered if they would even hear what she had to say, but Strauss told her not to worry.

Strauss got her to the podium, and the audience saw a film about her. When the lights came on, Jordan stood before them. She had lost sixty pounds, she had a new green suit, and she looked good. The crowd broke into applause.

Then Barbara Jordan began doing what she did best—speaking to people about what she believed in. She reminded them that Democrats had been meeting in convention for 144 years but that there was something different about the 1976 convention. "There is something special about tonight," she said. "What is different? What is special? I, Barbara Jordan, am a keynote speaker."

She reminded them of what their party stood for: "equality for all and privileges for none." And she told them that she, herself, was a symbol of the democracy that the Democratic party stood for.

When she finished, the crowd gave her a standing ovation that lasted five minutes. The band played "The Eyes of Texas," and the Texas delegation waved the Texas flag. To many, Barbara Jordan was the star of the Democratic convention.

The *New York Times* commented on Jordan, an African-American woman, and Strauss, a Jewish businessman, as leaders of the Democratic party and told Democrats, "You've come a long way, baby."

One reporter said, "She knew exactly how to bring this big motley hall into order and send a chill through the nation," while another congratulated Democrats for bringing "Barbara Jordan off the bench. Miss Jordan, as the ballplayers say, took it downtown. She tore it up. Grand slam."

Many expected Jordan to be President Jimmy Carter's running mate. The day after her speech people began wearing "Barbara Jordan for Vice President" buttons, and even the president's mother proudly wore one.

Jordan, however, knew it was not time for an African-American woman to be on the presidential ticket. When fellow members of the House of Representatives pushed her nomination, she would not let them enter her name. "It's not my turn," she told them. "When it's my turn, you'll know it."

However, Jordan had her heart set on becoming the attorney general of the United States, and she campaigned hard for Jimmy Carter. Although she had won a third term in Congress, everyone expected her to be part of the president's cabinet.

When President Carter talked to her, however, Jordan was not feeling well. When she expressed interest in the attorney general's job, Carter told her he had already picked someone else. Jordan was upset and left the meeting early. Friends and colleagues knew that the president had disappointed her.

She also was disappointed with what Congress could achieve. When the media asked if she planned to challenge Texan John Tower for his seat in the U.S. Senate in 1978, she had to make a decision.

She talked about the Senate seat with friends and advisers, and decided she could not win it. Her illness would prevent the active campaigning she had done in the past. The main point was that she felt she could get the Democratic nomination, but might well lose to a Republican.

Still she had important work to do in Congress, and she set about getting the job done. She worked to get the Civil Rights Act's Title VI extended to all federal programs and the Law Enforcement Administration Act renewed. Now state and local governments could not use federal funds to discriminate.

She was the member of the House who blocked one Senate bill from passing. It was a bill to split the Fifth Circuit Court of Appeals. This was the court that enforced civil rights laws, and the NAACP and other civil rights groups did not want the court split.

When they approached Jordan for help, she knew she would be opposing a powerful Senator, James Eastland. She knew she would have to go to members of the House to get support for her bill. Just how far would her aching legs take her?

Multiple sclerosis had taken its toll. Jordan had already withdrawn from many of the ceremonial functions of Congress. She just couldn't make it to many photographic sessions. She was tired and knew she had to make a decision. She had never intended to serve in Congress to the end of her life, but what was she to do?

Before she made her decision, however, she had to travel to Boston to get one more honor. And this was an important one. Harvard University had invited her to deliver its commencement address, the first African-American woman chosen for the honor. Also, she, along with the singer Marian Anderson and writer Eudora Welty, received honorary degrees.

She told Harvard graduates that what people wanted from their government was to be let in. Everyone should be included in the government of the United States.

After all, when she was a student at TSU, her debate coach had told her not to apply to Harvard. He thought she would never get in. Now, here she was. With her degree in hand, she couldn't have been prouder.

Professor Barbara Jordan and her students at the LBJ
School of Public Affairs
—courtesy of the Barbara Jordan Archives, Robert J. Terry Library,
Texas Southern University

Chapter 16

Teacher and Advisor

On December 10, 1977, Barbara Jordan called reporters to her office in the federal courthouse in Houston. She told them she did not plan to run for reelection. Her announcement stunned many. For them, she had united the African-American community. What would they do without her?

Jordan told them, she had not decided what she would do next. She needed to think about new opportunities, new options. What to do with the rest of her life.

But the first thing on her agenda was to relax and to enjoy life outside Washington. And she knew where she could do just that. She and her friend Nancy Earl had built a house in a beautiful section of Austin.

There among the trees, Jordan could relax, enjoy visits from her friends, "kick back," play her guitar, and sing. For once, the very public person had a private life.

She told reporters she would never cease to be a politician, but she would not be an active politician. She still was involved, however, with national issues and spoke out on the need for an Equal Rights Amendment to the Constitution. She was disappointed when the amendment failed in Congress.

She and the Austin author Shelby Hearon worked on a book about her life. *Barbara Jordan: A Self Portrait* was published in 1979, and she went on a book tour to promote it.

Then Don Kennard, a friend from her Senate years, suggested to the dean of the Lyndon Baines Johnson School of Public Affairs at the University of Texas at Austin that Jordan join the faculty. Jordan and Johnson had been great friends, and she liked the idea of teaching public policy to graduate students at the school that bore his name.

In January, 1979, Jordan began a new career as an academic. She would teach two classes. One would focus on the workings of state and national government and the other on political values and ethics. She began putting together lists of books for her students to read and visited the John F. Kennedy School at Harvard University to find out how others taught classes in ethics.

She found teaching as rewarding as politics. "When you teach students, you can see an immediate result of your efforts," she said. She would pose questions for her students, and they would discuss, debate, and defend their opinions. Just like Barbara Jordan had done in law school.

Now she was walking with a cane, but she still traveled giving speeches and became one of the few women to sit on boards of corporations. Texas Republican George Bush, later president of the United States, saw that she was offered her first directorship of a corporation.

By 1980, she was using a wheelchair more often, but used a motorized scooter to take her from her house to the patio. She enjoyed swimming in her pool and attending basketball games when the UT Lady Longhorns played.

Although she was no longer in the political spotlight, Americans had not forgotten Barbara Jordan and her remarkable voice. In 1984 the National Platform

Association named her the Best Living Orator and in 1985 served on a United Nations panel to study the role of corporations in South Africa and Namibia.

As a panel member, she traveled to South Africa to meet Nelson Mandela, and his daughter presented her with the first Nelson Mandela Award for Health and Human Rights.

She began to speak out once again on political issues and often appeared on talk shows about politics. When President Ronald Reagan appointed conservative Robert Bork to the Supreme Court, Jordan testified against him and he was defeated.

More honors came her way. Texan Bill Moyers had her discuss evil on television with poet Maya Angelou, and she wrote an essay for *Time* magazine on the women's movement. She appeared on radio and television and seconded the motion of fellow Texan Lloyd Bentsen for vice president of the United States.

Texas millionaire Ross Perot established a scholarship in her honor at the LBJ School, and she chose the person to receive the funds. Her first choice was a young woman from Houston's Fifth Ward, who had graduated from Texas Southern University.

Then, just as she was enjoying life to the fullest, tragedy struck. She exercised every day in her swimming pool, and one day her friend Nancy Earl found her floating in the pool. She was unconscious, and Nancy feared she had died.

Doctors saved her and told the press of her multiple sclerosis. They also told her she would be in a wheelchair for the rest of her life. But Barbara Jordan had a spirit that would not be broken. And she would continue to speak out on issues.

She campaigned for Michael Dukakis for president and spoke out against racism in America. "We are a divided people," she warned Americans. "We must let all

Americans be Americans regardless of where their ancestors were born."

She campaigned for Ann Richards for governor of Texas, and celebrated when Richards appointed women and minorities to state jobs. One of her appointments went to Barbara Jordan, who would serve as her unpaid ethics advisor.

Richards called for a strong ethics bill and told state legislators that if they failed to pass one, "I am going to have to face Barbara Jordan."

Then the governor of Arkansas called her to tell her he was running for president. Bill Clinton wanted Jordan to give one of the keynote speeches at the Democratic Convention. Jordan agreed and told Democrats that the "American Dream is not dead." She went on to remind them that, "This party will not tolerate bigotry . . . America's strength lies in its diversity."

When Bill Clinton was inaugurated as president, Barbara Jordan was his special guest. At the prayer service before the inauguration, a young African-American boy brought her his Bible to sign. When her aide asked about her signing it, she said, "He must have thought I wrote it."

Then President Clinton appointed Jordan to serve as chair of the Commission on Immigration Reform, and she worked with members to set a workable immigration policy. And the president went one step further. In 1994, he presented Barbara Jordan with the nation's highest honor, the Presidential Medal of Freedom. After the ceremony, the Marine Corps band struck up "The Eyes of Texas."

The woman who had begun work on immigration reform, however, did not live to see the end. She traveled to Mexico to meet with government officials on immigration problems, continued to teach classes, and advise Governor Richards.

After a visit with her family at Christmas, Jordan was looking forward to the first faculty meeting of the new semester. Then she had problems breathing and was rushed to the hospital. At 9:15 in the evening of January 16, 1996, she stopped breathing.

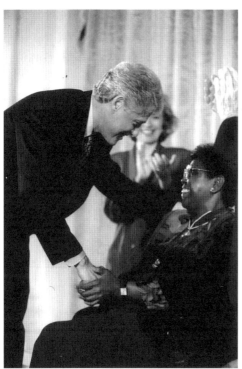

Former President Bill Clinton awards the Presidential Medal of Freedom to Barbara Jordan
—courtesy of the Barbara Jordan Archives, Robert J. Terry Library, Texas Southern University

The congregation of Good Hope Missionary Baptist Church, joined by President Clinton and Governor Ann Richards, celebrated her life on January 20. Reverend D.Z. Cofield said of her: "We can be the best we can be because she was the best she was."

Another memorial was held in Austin and then she was buried in the Texas State Cemetery, close to the Texas hero, Stephen F. Austin. For Barbara Jordan, it was yet another "first" in a lifetime of "firsts." She was the first African-American to be buried in her state's cemetery.

This portrait of Barbara Jordan hangs in the Texas
Senate Chamber
—courtesy of the Texas State Preservation Board

Chapter 17

Legacy

After Barbara Jordan's death, her life was celebrated in newspaper and magazine stories. Television news programs told of her life—a life dedicated to the cause of civil rights and support of the Constitution.

Schools were named in her honor, and her papers were brought home to Texas Southern University. People everywhere talked about this famous Texan, who had made her mark on the state and nation.

Rising from Houston's Fifth Ward to the Texas Senate and the Congress of the United States, she became a role model for many African-Americans—both women and men—a role model of how to do it and how to do it right.

Other African-American women followed in her footsteps to the Texas legislature. Many felt that it had been easier for them because Barbara Jordan had been "first."

As Texas enters the twenty-first century, its only two congresswomen are African-American. Sheilah Jackson Lee represents Houston's Eighteenth District, the district first represented by Jordan, while Eddie Bernice Johnson represents the Thirtieth Congressional District in Dallas. They are testaments to Jordan's paving the way to Washington.

When people visit the Texas Senate chambers in Austin, they can look at a fine portrait of Jordan. It honors the first African-American woman to sit in the Senate. An exhibit telling the story of her life is in the Visitors Center, east of the state capitol where she served. And when people speak of Texas politicians, all they have to say is "Barbara," and everyone knows whom they mean.

In a lifetime of "firsts," however, the accomplishment Barbara Jordan was proudest of was representing the people of Houston's Fifth Ward. "I have tried to represent them, and I've done that to the best of my ability."

Like everything she did, she did it with her mind, her heart, and her voice. She spoke countless words on behalf of civil rights and on behalf of all Americans. But the words that most Americans will remember her by are those spoken in support of the document that defines the United States of America—"My belief in the Constitution is whole. It is complete. It is total."

She is honored for her work in the United States Congress, and among Texas women, Barbara Jordan has gained an important first—first in the hearts of Texans.

Words to Know

Knowing the following words will help you understand the story of Barbara Jordan's life. Adding them to your reading and writing vocabulary will help you understand American history and government.

administration—officials in the executive branch of government

agenda—program of things to be done

amendment—change or addition made to a bill, law, or constitution

bigotry—prejudice

boycott—join together to force to action

caucus—leaders meeting to decide on policy or a course of action

civil rights—guaranteed to a person as a member of society

compromise—agreement where each party gives up a demand

congregation—assembly of people for religious worship

Congress—governing body of the nation; made up of Senate and House of Representatives

conservative—wants things to stay the same or for change to come slowly

Constitution—document that contains the form and structure of government

consumer group—people who buy or use products

corruption—bribery or other dishonest dealings

declamation—speech made in a forceful or dramatic manner

delegation—group chosen to act for or represent others

designate—to appoint or name to an office or duty

discrimination—showing prejudice against a group of peole

Emancipation Proclamation—act of President Lincoln's to free slaves during the Civil War

endorse—to support a candidate or issue

endowment fund—money set aside to support an institution

ethics—standards of moral conduct

exempt—not subject to a rule, law, or obligation

filibuster—long speeches made to keep a bill from passage

general election—nationwide or statewide election where voters choose between candidates of a political party

gestures—movement of the parts of the body; in speaking, hands making dramatic movements

impeach—bring charges of misconduct against a government official

integrate—bring together; to remove legal barriers that keep people apart

judicial—relating to the legal system or courts

keynote speaker—delivers the address that sets the theme of a convention

legacy—what one hands down to others

legislative district—area made up of voters who choose their legislators

legislature—governing body of state

liberal—one who believes in legislative action to meet individual needs

media—means of communication; radio, television, newspapers that provide the public with news and information

minimum wage—a sum set by a law that is the lowest amount a worker may earn
misdemeanor—minor legal offense

monitor—to watch or check

motley—a group of clashing people

multiple sclerosis—disease of the nervous system

NAACP—works for civil rights of African-Americans

nominate—to name as a candidate for election or position

option—choice

oratorical—having to do with a formal speech

orator—one who delivers a formal speech

ovation—enthusiastic outburst of applause or welcome

podium—a low platform for speakers

political activist—advances a cause; works in the political arena

poll tax—tax paid by people in order to vote

precinct—an area set off for the purpose of voting

primary election—voters of a political party nominate candidates for office

pro tem—serving for a specific time

protest march—group action for a cause or change
racism—says that one race is superior to another

redistricting—changing the boundary lines of a precinct or district

resolution—formal statement adopted by a group

sales tax—tax on products that people buy

segregation—separation of persons by color, race, or religion

sit-ins—taking a seat and remaining there; used by civil rights demonstrators

state's attorney—one who tries or defends legal cases for the state

welfare programs—give money and aid to people who cannot afford services

white primary—election where only Anglos can vote

worker's compensation—payment to a worker for an injury or disease suffered at work

Read More About Barbara Jordan

You might want to read more about this famous and important Texas woman. The following books will tell you more about this famous American:

For students:
Barnes, Marion E. *Black Texans: They Overcame*. Austin: Eakin Press, 1996.
Blue, Rose, et.al. *Barbara Jordan*. Broomwall, Pa.: Chelsea House, 1992.
Kelin, Norman and Sabra-Anne Kelin. *Barbara Jordan: Congresswoman*. New York: Holloway House, 1993.
Rhodes, Lisa Renee. *Barbara Jordan: Voice of Democracy*. Danbury, Ct.: Franklin Watts, 1998.

For teachers:
Crawford, Ann Fears and Crystal Sasse Ragsdale. *Women in Texas: Their Lives, Their Experiences, Their Accomplishments*. Austin: State House Press, 1972.
Jones, Nancy Baker and Ruthe Winegarten. *Capitol Women: Texas Women Legislators*. Austin: University of Texas Press, 2000.
Jordan, Barbara and Shelby Hearon. *Barbara Jordan: A Self-Portrait*. New York: Doubleday & Company, 1979.

Rogers, Mary Beth. *Barbara Jordan: American Hero.* New York: Bantam Books, 1998.

Winegarten, Ruthe, et.al. *Black Texas Women.* Austin: University of Texas Press, 1995.

About the Author

Ann Fears Crawford is the author of a number of books about Texas for both young readers and adults. You may have read her books, *New Life, New land: Women in Early Texas*; *Sam Houston: American Hero*; *Jane Long: Frontier Woman*; *Lizzie: Queen of the Cattle Trail*; *Rosa: A German Woman on the Texas Frontier*; and *Mary Maverick of Old San Antonio*.

In the 1970s, when she was teaching political science, a group of authors asked her to write a selection on Texas political women for a college textbook. Of course, she wrote about Barbara Jordan.

They turned down her selection saying that by the 1980s, "no one would remember Barbara Jordan." So that Texans would remember this remarkable woman, Crawford wrote about Barbara Jordan for the book, *Women in Texas*.

Everywhere she speaks people want to know about Barbara Jordan, so she wrote this book to help young readers remember this famous Texan.

Crawford's other books for adults are *Texas Women: Frontier To Future*; *Frankie: Mrs. R.D. Randolph and Texas Liberal Politics*, and *The Eagle: Santa Anna's Memoirs*.

She teaches both Texas and United States history at Community College.